Making a New Nation

COLONIAL AMERICA

Michael Burgan

HEINEMANN LIBRARY
CHICAGO, ILLINOIS

Designed by Philippa Baile and Kim Miracle
Maps by Jeff Edwards
Printed and bound in China by WKT company limited

11 10 09 08 07
10 9 8 7 6 5 4 3 2 1

Library of Congress Cataloging-in-Publication Data
Burgan, Michael.
  Colonial America / Michael Burgan.
     p. cm. -- (Making a new nation)
  Includes bibliographical references and index.
  ISBN 1-4034-7827-9 (library binding-hardcover) -- ISBN 1-4034-7834-1 (pbk.)
  1. United States--History--Colonial period, ca. 1600-1775--Juvenile literature.
I. Title. II. Series.
  E188 .B942006
  973.2--dc22

                          2006003247

Acknowledgments
The author and publisher are grateful to the following for permission to reproduce
copyright material: Art Resource, NY p. **12** (Aldo Tutino); Art Resource, NY/Smithsonian
American Art Museum, Washington, D.C. p. **25**; Colonial Williamsburg Foundation p. **38**;
Corbis pp. **14** (Nathan Benn), **18** (Roman Soumar), **24** (Dave Bartruff); Corbis/Bettmann
pp. **16**, **20**, **31**, **41**; Corbis/The Mariners' Museum p. **15**; Getty Images p. **34** (Gary
Randall); Getty Images/Hulton Archive pp. **8**, **33**, **40**; Library of Congress pp. **21**, **43**;
Lonely Planet p. **5** (Jim Wark); Northwind Picture Archives pp. **7**, **10**, **19**, **23**, **29**, **30**, **39**;
Painet Inc. p. **9**; St. Isaac Jogues, © 1988 Br. R. Lentz, ofm, Courtesy of Trinity Stores,
www.trinitystores.com, 800.699.4482 p. **22**; Stock Montage, Inc. p. **36**; The Granger
Collection, New York pp. **6**, **17**, **27**, **32**, **37**.

Cover photograph reproduced with the permission of The Granger Collection, New York.

The publishers would like to thank David Davidson of Northwestern University
 for his help in the preparation of this book.

Every effort has been made to contact copyright holders of any material reproduced in
this book. Any omissions will be rectified in subsequent printings if notice is given to
the publisher.

CONTENTS

Some words are shown in bold, **like this**. You can find
out what they mean by looking in the glossary.

A RACE FOR RICHES

During the 1400s and 1500s, better ships and sailing methods were developed. They made it easier for people to travel farther than they had ever traveled before. European rulers sent out **settlers** to start **colonies** in other lands. The rulers hoped the colonies would bring them great riches. Each country hoped to find valuable colonies before other countries did.

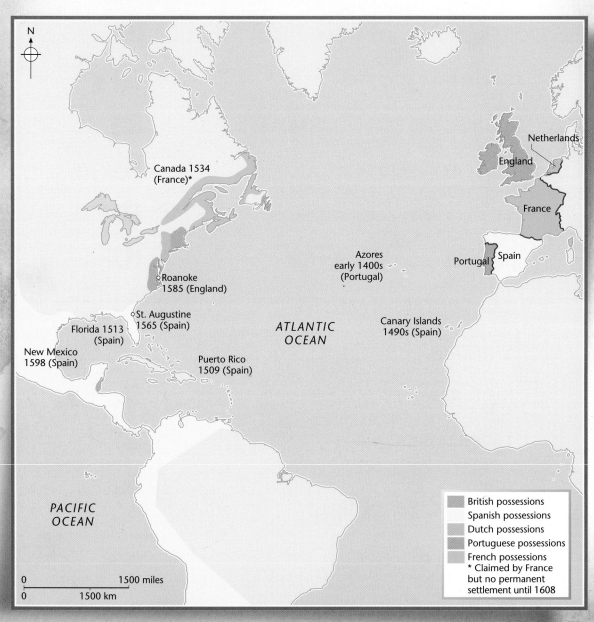

N

Canada 1534
(France)*

Netherlands

England

France

Azores
early 1400s
(Portugal)

Portugal   Spain

Roanoke
1585 (England)

St. Augustine
1565 (Spain)

ATLANTIC
OCEAN

Canary Islands
1490s (Spain)

Florida 1513
(Spain)

New Mexico
1598 (Spain)

Puerto Rico
1509 (Spain)

PACIFIC
OCEAN

British possessions
Spanish possessions
Dutch possessions
Portuguese possessions
French possessions
* Claimed by France
but no permanent
settlement until 1608

| 0 | | 1500 miles |
| 0 | 1500 km | |

*Europeans tried to start some of their first colonies
in North America along the Atlantic coast.*

COLONIES IN THE "NEW WORLD"

Europeans called North and South America the "New World." Spain and Portugal started the first colonies there. The Portuguese focused on Brazil, but the Spaniards explored a much larger region. In 1513 Spanish explorers landed in what is now Florida. They were looking for gold and silver, but they did not find much. They tried to start colonies along the Atlantic coast.

The Spanish colonies reached as far north as modern-day South Carolina. Most of these colonies failed. One reason they failed was because of problems with Native Americans. The Spanish forced Native Americans to give them food or to work as **slaves**. The Native Americans fought back to defend their lands and their way of life.

Despite the dangers, more Europeans came to North America. The French and British started colonies along the Atlantic coast, as far north as Canada. The Spanish also moved from Mexico into what is now New Mexico. During the 1600s, the Europeans built lasting colonies in what is now the United States.

The "lost colony"

In 1585 the first English settlers reached North America. They landed on an island near what is now North Carolina. They called their new home Roanoke. The Roanoke colony did not survive. Its leader, John White, went back to Europe for supplies. When he returned to Roanoke in 1590, all the settlers were gone. To this day, no one knows what happened to them.

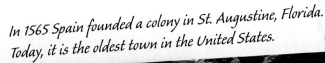

In 1565 Spain founded a colony in St. Augustine, Florida. Today, it is the oldest town in the United States.

NORTHERN SETTLEMENTS

Starting in 1598, the French began to build small trading forts in Canada. The only place that started as a French **settlement** that still exists today is Quebec. French rulers did not try to create a large colony that could support itself. Their goal was to make money by trading for beaver furs with the local Native Americans.

In the 1600s, the French traded from Quebec with Native Americans who lived in what is now New York. The Dutch were the first Europeans to settle in this area, which they called New Netherland. In 1614 the Dutch built a fort on an island in the Hudson River, near what is now Albany, New York. They also traded with the Native Americans for furs. A few years later, the Dutch founded the town of New Amsterdam at the mouth of the Hudson River.

Beaver furs from North America were used to make hats and clothing in Europe.

Virginia tobacco, which was transported in large barrels, was often used as money.

THE FIRST ENGLISH COLONIES

In 1607 the English founded the colony of Jamestown in Virginia. About 100 people lived there at first. Within a few years, they were growing tobacco, a crop that the Native Americans first raised. Europe did not have the right **climate** to grow tobacco. Virginia's settlers began to make a lot of money growing tobacco and selling it in England.

In 1620 English settlers known as the Pilgrims landed in Plymouth, Massachusetts. Like other settlers, they hoped to make money selling furs and other resources. But the Pilgrims also wanted to worship as they chose. Soon after the Pilgrims came, a group of settlers called the Puritans founded the Massachusetts Bay Colony. They shared some of the Pilgrims' religious beliefs.

Wampum
Beside furs, the English and Dutch also traded with Native Americans for wampum. These white and purple beads made from clamshells were strung into belts. Wampum belts were religious items. They were also a form of money for both the tribes and the settlers.

WHY COLONISTS CAME TO AMERICA

Some English people wanted to **emigrate** to North America because of the **economy** in their homeland. Most people could not afford to own land in England. These people did not expect to become rich in North America. They merely wanted land for themselves and their families. They often had to work hard to get it.

Some poor or homeless people were taken off the streets of London and forced to go to Virginia.

THE ROLE OF RELIGION

Religious beliefs also drove settlers to the colonies. In England the Puritans and Pilgrims faced many problems. They could not openly practice their religion or serve in the government. Many Puritans and Pilgrims left England because they wanted to create their own governments based on their religious beliefs.

Religion also played a role in bringing settlers to Maryland. The founder of that colony was George Calvert, a Roman Catholic. Other Catholics from England also settled there. Roman Catholics from France and Spain wanted to spread their faith to the New World. They set up **missions** to teach Native Americans about their faith.

OTHER FACTORS

Relations between people also led some settlers to emigrate. The first settlers wrote letters to friends and family about the colonies. Colonial leaders also wrote letters and articles praising life in the New World. These writings were like today's ads. They convinced some Europeans to make the trip to North America.

One of the leaders of the Jamestown colony, John Smith, wanted to convince people to settle in New England. In 1616 he wrote, "The ground is so **fertile** that doubtless it is capable of producing any grain, fruits, or seeds you will sow or plant . . . All sorts of cattle may be bred here and fed in the islands . . . safely for nothing."

Emigration and the law

For some settlers, legal trouble led them to North America. Some people who had broken the law agreed to work in the colonies rather than go to jail in their homelands. Others went if they were wanted for a crime or owed money. Emigrating let them avoid people who were chasing them.

The Spanish built the San Agustin de la Isleta Mission in New Mexico in 1612.

SLAVERY IN NORTH AMERICA

Some people who went to the New World did not choose to move there. Colonial leaders faced a problem because at first, not enough settlers wanted to move to the New World. There were not enough people to do the work. Because they needed more workers, Europeans forced people to come to the New World and work for them. Slaves mined metals and raised crops. Slaves were forced to do whatever their masters demanded.

Europeans first used Native Americans who were already living in North America as slaves. The Native Americans, however, often died from diseases the settlers brought with them. Early in the 1500s, Europeans began forcing people to travel from Africa to the Americas to work as slaves.

European traders purchased African slaves at large forts called slave factories and then transported them to the New World.

AFRICAN SLAVES

The Spanish brought African slaves to Florida and the Carolinas. In 1619 Africans reached Virginia. These Africans, however, may have actually been indentured servants (see right). In 1636 traders from Massachusetts began traveling to Africa to buy slaves. Toward the end of the 1600s, slavery grew in all the English colonies. Many African slaves worked on southern farms, where they grew tobacco, rice, sugar, and other crops. Slaves were not free, and they had few legal rights.

Many white Europeans looked down on Africans because of their dark skin. They also thought their own Christian faiths were the only true religions. These reasons meant that many white people thought they had a right to force Africans to be slaves, and to treat them as their property.

Indentured servants

Indentured servants were white or black people who signed a contract with a master. They agreed to work for the master for up to seven years. In return, their master usually paid for their trip to the colonies and gave them food and shelter. Masters also had almost complete control over the lives of indentured servants, just as they did with slaves. However, masters had to give the servants land, tools, or clothing when their contracts ended.

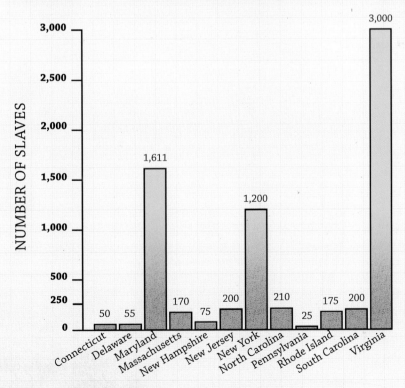

SLAVES IN THE ENGLISH COLONIES IN 1680

NUMBER OF SLAVES

Connecticut: 50
Delaware: 55
Maryland: 1,611
Massachusetts: 170
New Hampshire: 75
New Jersey: 200
New York: 1,200
North Carolina: 210
Pennsylvania: 25
Rhode Island: 175
South Carolina: 200
Virginia: 3,000

There were thousands of slaves already living in America by the end of the 1600s.

THE ORIGINAL SETTLERS

Native Americans were the first people in North America. They began arriving in what is now Alaska from Asia about 15,000 years ago. Hundreds of tribes existed when Christopher Columbus reached the New World in 1492. Several million Native Americans then lived in what became the United States.

In the decades after Columbus, the Spanish moved into southern Florida. One of the major tribes there was the Calusa. Along the coast, they built islands out of seashells. Their homes were open platforms on top of poles. The Calusa fished and hunted for food. At first, the Calusa fought the Spanish. After a while, however, they realized that the Spanish had better weapons.

Skilled Calusa craftsmen carved items out of wood, such as this statue of a panther.

NATIVE AMERICANS OF THE SOUTHWEST

In the Southwest, the Spanish met native people they called the Pueblo. These Native Americans lived in villages, which the Spanish called *pueblos*. The Pueblo buildings were made out of **adobe**. One large adobe building might have dozens of apartments in which hundreds of people lived.

The Pueblo were actually many different Native American tribes with different languages. The tribes, however, shared a lifestyle based on farming. Their main crops were corn, beans, and squash. The Pueblo also hunted for meat.

Deadly diseases

Along with their weapons, the Europeans brought an even greater deadly force to the New World: disease. Native Americans had never been exposed to diseases such as smallpox, the flu, and measles. Their bodies did not have the natural defenses needed to fight these illnesses. Some tribes lost up to half their members as European diseases spread among them. In 1616, an outbreak of disease killed many Native Americans in the East.

With the contact between Europe and the Americas, the two regions discovered new things to trade.

THE ATLANTIC EXCHANGE

What the Native Americans Received	What the Europeans Received
alcohol	chili pepper
cattle	cocoa
chicken	corn
coffee	peanut
guns	potato
horses	pumpkin
iron goods (pots, tools)	squash
pigs	tobacco
rice	tomato
sugar	wampum
wheat	

EASTERN WOODLAND NATIVE AMERICANS

Along the Atlantic coast, European settlers met many different Native American tribes. Together, all the tribes living in North America from the Atlantic coast to the Mississippi River became known as the Eastern Woodland Native Americans.

In the Northeast, most tribes spoke languages called Algonquian and Iroquoian. Algonquian tribes lived from Maine to Virginia. The Wampanoag were the Algonquian tribe that greeted the Pilgrims when they reached Plymouth. Another well-known Algonquian tribe was the Pequot. The main Iroquois tribes were the Cayuga, Mohawk, Oneida, Onondoga, and Seneca. They were often called the Five Nations. These tribes lived in New York and traded furs with French and Dutch settlers.

The Algonquian and Iroquois tribes spent part of the year farming and part of the year hunting. One difference between the two groups was their homes. Many families of Iroquois lived together in large, bark-covered homes called longhouses. Algonquian tribes usually built smaller, dome-shaped homes called wigwams.

An Iroquois longhouse could be more than 100 feet (30.5 meters) long and 18 feet (5.5 meters) wide. One longhouse house might hold up to ten families.

EASTERN WOODLAND TRIBES OF THE SOUTHEAST

From the Carolinas to Florida, many Eastern Woodland tribes spoke Muskogean or Siouan languages. These tribes included the Choctaw and Chickasaw. They lived farther inland than their northern neighbors. So did the Cherokee, who spoke an Iroquoian language. The main contact between these tribes and European settlers came in the 1700s. Tribes in this region mostly relied on farming to survive. As with other Native Americans, they also hunted, gathered, and fished.

Tribes in Virginia, such as the Secotan, sometimes grilled the fish they caught.

Indian life

Johannes Megapolensis was a Dutch minister who spent time with the Mohawk. Here is some of what he wrote about them in 1644: "They make themselves stockings and also shoes of deer skin. . . . The women, as well as the men, go with their heads bare. . . . They smear their heads with bear's-grease . . . they say they do it to make their hair grow better and to prevent their having **lice**."

THE COLONISTS AND NATIVE AMERICANS

Native Americans did not worship the Christian God. **Missionaries converted** some to Christianity, but most Europeans never saw these converts as equal to whites. Native Americans and Europeans also had different ideas about land. Europeans often paid tribes for land. The settlers then thought they owned the land. Most tribes, however, did not think people could own land. It was for all people to share. The Native Americans were only allowing the Europeans to use the land. They still expected to use it as well. The settlers upset the Native Americans by putting up fences and telling them they could no longer hunt on the land.

NATIVE AMERICAN WARS

In some places, settlers also expected local tribes to sell them food. The Native Americans often only had enough crops for themselves. In Jamestown, the settlers' need for food led to conflicts with the Powhatan. In 1609 the first of several major wars erupted in Virginia. Over the next few decades, the colonists' population grew and they were able to defeat the Powhatan and take more of their land.

In New England, the first major Native American war came in 1637. The Puritans, Pilgrims, and some Native American **allies** battled the Pequot. The settlers destroyed the main Pequot village, and survivors were made to work as slaves.

Opechancanough, a Powhatan chief, led his people in several wars against settlers in Virginia.

NATIVE AMERICAN FRIENDSHIPS

Relations between the colonists and Native Americans were sometimes peaceful. Tribes often wanted to buy settlers' goods. Sometimes they needed help fighting enemy tribes. In many cases, settlers needed the Native Americans' help to survive. The tribes showed the colonists how to plant local crops and where to hunt and fish.

Friend to the Pilgrims

In 1621 the Pilgrims of Plymouth met a Native American named Tisquantum. He had been captured by an English sailor and then sold into slavery in Spain. Tisquantum escaped and fled to London before returning to his home in Massachusetts. Tisquantum showed the Pilgrims how to plant corn. Tisquantum also led the settlers on trading trips.

*Massasoit, the chief of the Wampanoag, signed a **treaty** of friendship in 1621 with Governor John Carver of Plymouth.*

EARLY COLONIAL LIFE

The colonists in North America faced hard lives. Not only did they have to produce enough food to survive, but they also had to build their settlements from scratch. During the 1600s, the English had the most colonists in North America. The first colonists had brought some important items with them from England. These included tools, seeds, farm animals, and weapons.

The Pilgrims and Puritans were mostly farmers. They were lucky to find some fields already cleared, thanks to the Native Americans who had lived there before them. In other areas, settlers had to cut down trees and move rocks before they could farm. In the southern colonies, most English farmers grew **cash crops** as well their own food. Landowners then sold or traded the cash crops for other items they needed.

Settlers in New England built simple homes like the ones they had in England.

STAYING IN TOUCH

The first English settlements were near water. Boats and ships provided the best way to transport people and goods. Ships also carried letters and other documents between the colonies and Europe. These helped the colonists stay in touch and feel connected to their homeland. The colonists still had relationships with leaders from their home countries. They also set up their own governments to deal with local problems.

Overseas trade

Families tried to meet their needs by making many items, such as clothing, butter, and furniture. But for many decades, the settlers bought many household items from overseas. The colonists shipped tobacco, furs, timber, and fish to England and other colonies in the New World. In return, they received foods that they could not grow, such as sugar and tea. The colonists also traded for manufactured goods, such as tools, kitchen items, and cloth.

In the colonies, women raised children and took care of the home. One common chore was spinning wool into yarn.

THE FRONTIER

The first English colonists in North America claimed the best farmland that was available near the Atlantic coast. By the 1660s, new arrivals had to move into the **frontier** to find land.

Frontier life was hard. Settlers there often lived far apart from each other, and there were few roads. The ones that did exist were in poor shape, so travel was slow. The frontier settlers had no easy way to stay in touch with people in the colonial towns or England. They also had to spend more time and money getting their goods to market.

Frontier settlers were in more danger of violence. They sometimes argued with Native Americans over the use of land. If fighting broke out, the settlers were too far from the main towns to receive much help. That distance also hurt the frontier settlers in **politics**. They could not influence the colonial rulers. The governments often ignored their calls for protection or to lower taxes.

French traders and European settlers learned how to make canoes from the Native Americans.

THE FRENCH EXPERIENCE ON THE FRONTIER

The first French fur traders slowly moved out of their main base in Canada. They headed into New York and the upper Midwest. During the 1660s, a group of French traders emerged in these frontier areas. These traders traveled alone or in small groups to distant Native American villages to obtain furs. Many of them learned the languages of the tribes they met. Some also married Native American women and made allies with their tribes.

Located in New Jersey, this 1600s home is the oldest surviving log cabin in North America.

Log cabins

From 1638 to 1655, Sweden had a small colony in North America. It was called New Sweden and was located along the Delaware River. Settlers there were the first Americans to build log cabins. Most of these cabins were built without using any nails. Notches cut into the logs and wooden pins kept the houses together.

RELIGIOUS LIFE

In the 1600s, religion was an important part of daily life. There were people of many different faiths in the colonies. Most European nations had one official religion supported by the government. Some American colonies also followed this pattern. In New England, non-**Protestants** could not worship in public, and everyone was expected to attend church on Sundays.

Roman Catholics, on the other hand, settled in Maryland. In 1649 a law in that colony let all Christians worship as they chose. The Dutch in New Netherland also favored freedom for people of all religions to worship as they chose. Since New Netherland had a shortage of workers, the colony accepted members of many faiths.

Isaac Joques was a French missionary. He was the first Roman Catholic priest known to enter New Netherland.

THE MISSIONARIES

By 1628 Spain had several dozen missions in New Mexico. The missionaries forced the Native Americans to give up their old faith, clothing, and language. The tribes did not have much choice, since the missions also had soldiers. The Native Americans often had to accept the demands of the missions or be killed. French missionaries traveled from Canada into New York and other areas to teach Native Americans about the Catholic religion.

Church and state

In 1636 the Puritans' strict religious beliefs drove Roger Williams out of Massachusetts Bay. He then founded the colony of Rhode Island. Unlike the Puritans, Williams wanted to separate the church and state. He did not want the government to pass laws that limited people's rights to worship as they chose.

In Puritan New England, criminals were sometimes locked into wooden stocks as punishment for their crimes.

Settlers in New York

In 1654 Jews fleeing violence in Brazil, in South America, were allowed to settle in New Amsterdam. Today, this town is New York City. These were the first Jewish settlers in North America. New York remains a major Jewish population center in the United States.

SPANISH AND FRENCH EXPANSION

Starting in the 1690s, the Spanish began to move farther into New Mexico. They built missions and forts in what is now Texas and Arizona. In the last half of the 1700s, missionaries entered California. They built a string of missions along the Pacific coast. During this time, Mexico remained Spain's most valuable colony in North America. Spanish leaders kept only enough soldiers and settlers in New Mexico to keep out other Europeans. By the mid-1700s, the two largest settlements in New Mexico were Santa Fe and El Paso. Each had less than 3,000 people. By that time, Boston, New York, and Philadelphia each had more than 10,000 people.

In 1769 Father Junípero Serra founded Spain's first mission in California, in San Diego.

Tribes of the Great Plains hunted buffalo for their meat and hides and used their bones for tools.

LIVING ALONGSIDE NATIVE AMERICANS

The Spanish were more interested in converting Native Americans than in trading with them. Even so, the Spanish and other Europeans did some trading with these tribes. The Europeans wanted to trade for fur and animal skins. In return, the Native Americans received cloth, metal tools, and guns. Sometimes Native Americans and the Spanish colonies also fought.

The Spanish brought horses with them to the New World. The Native Americans of the Great Plains came to value these animals for their speed and power. Using horses and guns, the Native Americans of the Plains had an easier time hunting buffalo. These large animals were their main source of meat. During the 1700s, tribes such as the Apache and Comanche became wealthy by trading buffalo products with the Europeans. But over time, most of the buffalo were killed.

A northern colony

Starting in the 1700s, Russian fur traders came to Alaska. In 1784 the Russians built their first permanent colony there, at Kodiak Island. For a brief time, the Russians also had a fort in northern California.

SETTLING LOUISIANA

During the 1680s, the French claimed a large area that it called Louisiana. It lay east of New Mexico and included the Mississippi River. The French wanted to build a string of forts along the Gulf of Mexico and the Mississippi River. They would then control shipping from Canada to the Gulf of Mexico. The first successful settlement in Louisiana was Biloxi, in present-day Mississippi.

In the colony's first years, few people came to Louisiana. The climate was much hotter than in Europe, and diseases were common. "Numbers died of misery or disease, and the country was emptied as rapidly as it had filled," wrote Pierre de Charlevoix, a French priest. Also, French laws limited who could settle in French colonies. To draw more settlers, the government finally changed those laws. For the first time, people who were not Roman Catholics could live in French colonies. Several thousand German Protestants then settled in Louisiana. The colony's leaders soon brought in African slaves. By 1746 Louisiana had more slaves than white settlers.

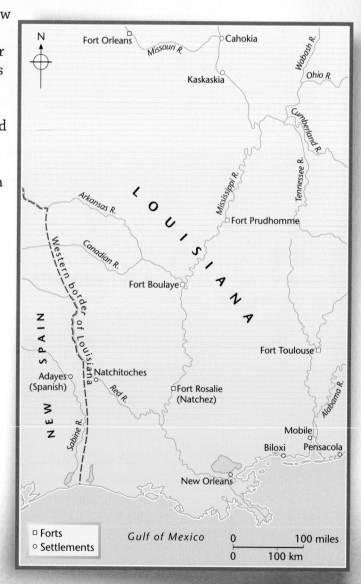

This map shows major French settlements in Louisiana and the Midwest around 1750.

NEW ORLEANS

In 1718 the French founded New Orleans. This city was located along the Mississippi River. It soon became the colony's capital and major city. Residents in and around New Orleans grew their own food. They also raised tobacco and **indigo** as cash crops. The climate, however, made farming difficult. For these settlers, trading with the Native Americans for deerskin was a bigger source of money.

Louisiana law

Unlike English settlers, the settlers of Louisiana did not elect their own local government officials. A governor chosen by the king of France handled military affairs and foreign relations. Other French officials handled money matters. The leaders of Louisiana were often **corrupt** and stole money and supplies. Every year, France poured more money into Louisiana than it made there. It kept control of the colony anyway, to make sure the English or Spanish did not take it.

Four years after it was founded, New Orleans became the capital of Louisiana.

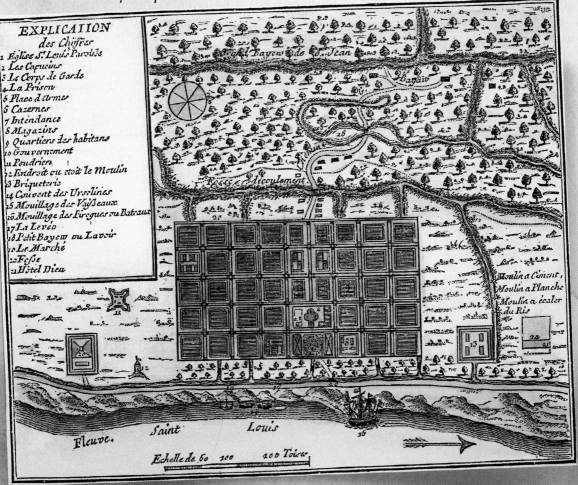

WARS OF CONQUEST

The colonial period was a time of many wars and battles. European nations sometimes argued over the **borders** of their North American colonies. Sometimes these arguments led to war. Other times, wars between European nations came to North America. Sometimes these conflicts would involve Native Americans, too.

One war that started up in the 1600s was between the Dutch and English. Starting in the 1650s, the Dutch and English fought a series of wars at sea and in Africa. In 1664 the English brought the war to the New World. An English fleet sailed into New Amsterdam and demanded that the Dutch surrender. The Dutch did not have many troops, so they agreed. The English took control of New Netherland and renamed it New York. New Amsterdam became New York City.

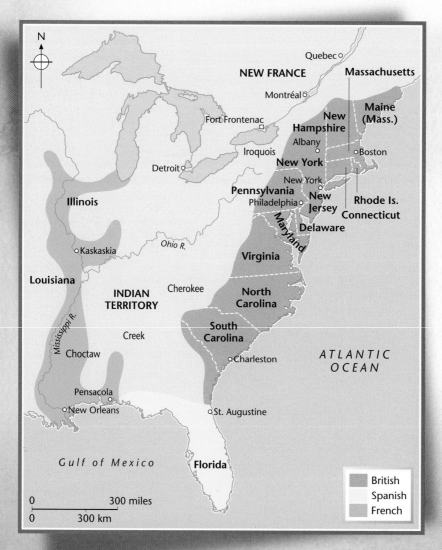

By 1690 England had colonies along the Atlantic coast from the Carolinas to Maine.

KING PHILIP'S WAR

Since the Pequot War of 1637, colonists in New England had experienced few problems with the Native Americans. In 1675, however, the Wampanoag and their allies launched a war against settlers in Connecticut, Massachusetts, and Rhode Island. The Wampanoag leader was Metacom. The English called him King Philip. His father, Massasoit, had been friendly with the colonists. But Metacom had grown angry with them as his tribe lost more of its land and its legal rights. For several months, Metacom and his warriors raided English towns. The colonists and their Native American allies finally defeated the Wampanoag. None of the tribes in the region ever challenged the colonists again.

Raiders

During King Philip's War, Mary Rowlandson was captured during a Native American raid. Later, she wrote about some of what she saw: "Hearing the noise of some guns, we looked out; several houses were burning . . . there were five persons taken in one house; the father and the mother and a [young] child they knocked on the head; the other two they took and carried away alive."

Metacom was killed in 1676. Most surviving Wampanoag were sold into slavery.

WARS IN THE NORTH

Starting in 1690, French and English colonists fought a series of wars in the Northeast. Each side relied on local tribes for help. The English colonists called the first conflict King William's War. French and Native American raiders attacked Schenectady, New York. Most of the residents were either killed or captured. The English fought back by invading Canada. For several years, the two sides attacked each other along their shared border. In 1698 France and England finally declared peace.

During Queen Anne's War (1702–1713), American colonists and English troops seized Acadia, the land that is now Nova Scotia. The English let the French keep Cape Breton, an island off of Acadia. However, in King George's War (1740–1748), New Englanders helped the British take Cape Breton as well.

During the raid on Schenectady, 60 residents were killed and 80 were taken prisoner.

Charleston, South Carolina, became the largest city of England's southern colonies.

BATTLES IN THE SOUTH

The English also fought the Spanish in North America. By the 1670s, the English had started to settle Carolina. This colony was south of Virginia. Its land included present-day North and South Carolina and part of Georgia. From their base in Florida, Spanish soldiers attacked the first English settlements in Carolina. The Spanish, however, failed to drive off the new colonists.

The English began to trade with the Native Americans of the region. They also used Native Americans to help defeat their enemies. Starting in the 1680s, the English encouraged the Native Americans to raid Spanish missions and forts. Eventually, English settlers drove the Spanish out of South Carolina. In 1732 the English founded Georgia as a separate colony. The first settlers arrived in 1733.

Slave trade in the Carolinas

The fighting in the Carolinas was partly tied to slavery. Native Americans raided neighboring Spanish villages and enslaved the people. They then traded the slaves to the English for guns. Since the Carolina colonists needed slaves, they welcomed this arrangement. The English also hired Native Americans to track down African slaves who ran away from their owners.

THE FRENCH AND INDIAN WAR

During the 1750s, the conflict between the French and British in North America reached its peak. France claimed the Ohio, the land west of the Allegheny Mountains up to the Ohio River. Great Britain also hoped to settle this region. To keep British colonists out, the French began building forts in western Pennsylvania. In 1753 George Washington was sent in to tell the French to leave. They refused. The next year, Washington, his men, and some Native American allies returned to the Ohio country. They fought the French and their local allies.

In 1755 several thousand British soldiers marched into the Ohio country to fight the French. Combined French and Native American forces defeated the British in western Pennsylvania. This was the first major battle of the French and Indian War. For several years, Native Americans attacked American colonists in Virginia, Maryland, and Pennsylvania. At the same time, the French captured British forts in New York. Finally, in 1759, the British defeated the French just outside the town of Quebec.

During the French and Indian War, the British forced French citizens out of Acadia, Canada. They eventually settled in Louisiana.

RESULTS OF THE WAR

The British victory in Canada ended the French and Indian War in North America. However, fighting continued in Europe, and the war did not officially end until 1763. Great Britain took all of France's lands in North America, except two small islands. The French had already given Louisiana to Spain. They could not afford to keep a colony there. With their victory, the British had greatly expanded their empire in North America.

From England to Britain
In 1707 England and Scotland united to form the Kingdom of Great Britain. From then on, American colonists were British citizens. The American colonies flew the new British flag, called the Union Jack.

George Washington was just 21 years old when he entered the Ohio to fight the French during the French and Indian War.

LIFE IN THE ENGLISH COLONIES

By 1763, when the French and Indian War finally ended, the map of North America looked very different than it had in 1700. The colonies had many towns and growing cities. On average, the colonists were among the wealthiest people in the world. More of them were starting to think of themselves as Americans.

Faneuil Hall, which opened in 1742 and still stands today, was an important marketplace in Boston.

LIVING IN NEW ENGLAND

New Englanders had many ways to make money. Fishing, shipbuilding, and trade remained important industries for the region. Merchants shipped goods to other British colonies in North America and the **West Indies**, as well as to Great Britain. The colonists continued to buy manufactured items from England. The area also developed its own industry. For example, **foundries** produced iron that local craftsmen turned into tools and other goods.

New England had fewer slaves than other parts of America, since it did not have many large **plantations**. But some New England ship owners and traders made fortunes bringing slaves into North America. They also bought goods produced on southern plantations and sold New England goods to the plantation owners. Many successful New England merchants built large homes and imported expensive goods for themselves. These items included fine dishes and clothes.

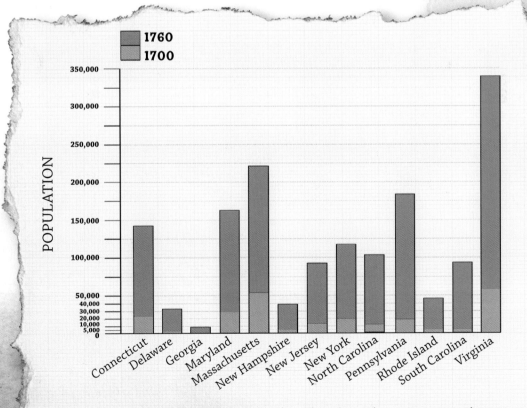

This graph shows the population growth in the colonies between 1700 and 1760.

THE MIDDLE COLONIES

South of New England were the middle colonies: New York, New Jersey, and Pennsylvania. The middle colonies were sometimes called the "breadbasket" of colonial America. Farmers in Pennsylvania and New York produced large amounts of grains and meat. In New York City, mills turned wheat into flour. Raw sugar bought in the West Indies was turned into sugar used in food. In Pennsylvania, workers built ships and made cloth for clothing. Businessmen in Philadelphia grew wealthy selling the many goods produced in the colony.

German immigrants in Pennsylvania developed the Conestoga wagon. This wagon helped carry goods and settlers to the North American frontier.

LAND OF DIVERSITY

In most colonies, settlers came from Great Britain. But the middle colonies had a larger number of residents who came from a number of different countries. Many German immigrants settled in Pennsylvania, and they had newspapers printed in their own language. Residents of the region also practiced a wide range of religions. Quakers had also settled Pennsylvania and parts of New Jersey. These Protestants believed everyone should worship as they chose. New York continued the old Dutch practice of allowing freedom of religion.

As in New England, slavery was not a huge part of daily life in the middle colonies. Still, New York had a sizable African-American slave population. New York City was a center for the slave trade.

Kinds of colonies

At one point, all three middle colonies were proprietary colonies, meaning that one person or a small group of people owned the land. The landowners had great control over the settlers. New York and New Jersey eventually became royal colonies. This meant the British ruler owned the land and chose the governors. The third kind of North American colony was the charter colony. The British government gave **investors** a document called a charter. The investors controlled the land for the king and set up rules for the colonists.

By the 1770s, Philadelphia was the largest and richest city in North America.

THE SOUTH

The southern colonies had two regions. Virginia, Maryland, and Delaware formed the Chesapeake, which bordered Chesapeake Bay. Farther south was the "low country" of the Carolinas and Georgia. Both areas relied heavily on slaves to grow cash crops.

Most planters of the Chesapeake grew tobacco. Growing tobacco drained **nutrients** from the soil. The land lost its ability to produce crops. This forced planters to move westward to find new land. Some larger Chesapeake plantations were like independent towns. The slaves on them raised food for themselves and their masters as well as tobacco. Skilled slaves also served as carpenters, blacksmiths, and furniture makers.

The main house at Carter's Grove, one of the largest plantations in Virginia, took over fifteen years to build.

THE LOW COUNTRY

In the low country, planters grew rice and indigo. Plantations there were usually larger than the ones in the Chesapeake, since growing rice required large areas of land and a lot of labor. The planters needed many slaves to work on these large farms. After 1720 the low-country colonies had twice as many African Americans, mostly slaves, as they did whites.

As in the North, not all southern slaves grew crops. Some worked as household servants or in small factories. And not all southern whites owned slaves. Many could not afford them, or did not own enough land to need slave labor.

During the 1700s, almost 100,000 slaves entered Charleston, South Carolina, and were sold at slave markets.

TO BE SOLD by William Yeomans, (in Charles Town Merchant,) a parcel of good Plantation Slaves. Encouragement will be given by taking Rice in Payment, or any Timber saddles and Furniture, choice Barbados and Boston Rum, also Cordial Waters and Limejuice, as well as a parcel of extraordinary Indian trading Goods, and many of other sorts suitable for the Season. a Time Credit, Security to be given if required There's likewise to be sold, very good Troopleg

Slave codes

Starting in the early 1700s, Virginia introduced the first slave code. The laws in the code restricted what slaves could do. Other southern colonies soon came up with their own codes. The Virginia code said slaves could never carry a weapon or travel without their master's written permission. The slave code also said that if slaves misbehaved, their masters could kill them and not go to jail. Most masters, however, avoided killing slaves. They did not want to lose what they saw as valuable property.

THE AMERICAN REVOLUTION

In 1763 most Americans were happy being British colonists. They had built a strong economy and enjoyed a long tradition of electing local leaders—although many people could not vote.

Many Americans were proud to help Great Britain win the French and Indian War. Soon after, however, the British decided to place new taxes on the Americans, leaving many people surprised and angry. In 1765 colonists protested violently when **Parliament** passed the Stamp Act. This law taxed papers used in the colonies. British citizens had a right to shape tax laws through the **representatives** they elected to Parliament. Americans claimed that Great Britain could not tax them because they did not have their own representatives in Parliament.

The British **repealed** the Stamp Act, but they placed new taxes on the colonies with the Townshend Acts of 1767. Merchants in Massachusetts and Virginia protested the Townshend Acts. They **boycotted** British goods. Boston became the center of protest against the British policies.

In 1770 fights between British soldiers and Boston residents led to the Boston Massacre. Five colonists were killed when soldiers opened fire on a crowd.

INDEPENDENCE

In 1773 Boston **patriots** protested a tax on tea by throwing crates of tea into the harbor. The British then shut down the government in Massachusetts. They sent a military governor to run the colony. In April 1775, British troops in Massachusetts clashed with colonial forces. This fighting started the American Revolution. Colonial leaders came to believe that America had the economic strength to survive on its own. In 1776 the Americans officially declared their independence.

The Proclamation of 1763

King George III of Great Britain feared a war between colonists and Native American tribes. He knew the colonists wanted tribal lands along the frontier. The king issued the Proclamation of 1763. It said the acolonists could not settle west of the Allegheny Mountains. Many Americans ignored the proclamation, which sometimes led to fighting along the frontier.

Battles between British troops and colonists during the American Revolution started with one at Lexington and Concord in 1775.

THE COURSE OF THE WAR

The main action of the American Revolution began in New England. It then spread into the middle colonies. The British used New York City as their main base. For a time, they also controlled Philadelphia, which was the American capital for most of the war. Starting in 1779, most of the fighting shifted to the South. Many key battles were fought in the Carolinas.

For most of the war, the Americans received aid from the French. In October 1781, French ships and soldiers helped the Americans defeat the British at Yorktown, Virginia. After this loss, British leaders decided to end the war and give the Americans their independence.

After the war, the United States grew. This map shows the United States in 1787.

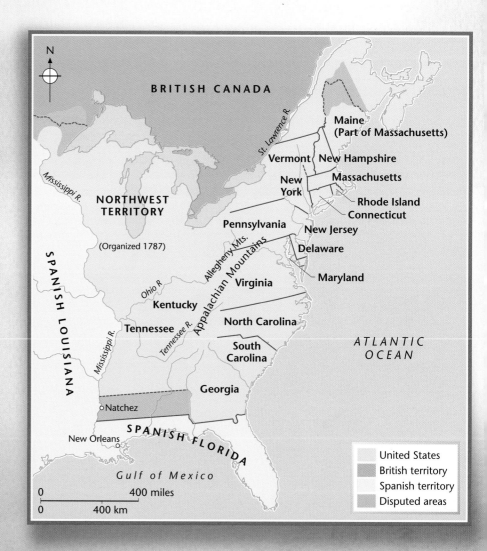

VICTORY AT LAST

The American Revolution officially ended in September 1783. In the peace treaty, the British officials gave the Americans more land than they had won during the war. In return, the Americans had to return land they had seized from people who supported the British. The British hoped that a growing United States would buy more British goods. The U.S. borders now stretched to the Mississippi River and Lake Superior. In 1787 **Congress** created the Northwest Territory in the new lands north of the Ohio River. Settlers would soon begin pouring into this land. The United States was now independent, and in control of its own destiny. It would continue to grow.

Fighting in the Old Northwest

Not all of the fighting in the American Revolution took place in the thirteen colonies. A patriot named George Rogers Clark led American forces in what is now called the Old Northwest. This region was west of Pennsylvania and north of the Ohio River. In July 1778, the Americans took the town of Kaskaskia, in what is now Illinois. From there, they moved on to the British fort at Vincennes. The British retook Vincennes that fall, but in February 1779, Clark once again captured the fort. The region around Vincennes remained under American control for the rest of the war.

General George Washington, who led the American Army from June 1775 until December 1783, accepted the British surrender at Yorktown in 1781.

TABLE OF THE COLONIES

COLONY	FOUNDED BY	YEAR
Connecticut	England	1633

FAST FACTS Several small, independent settlements of English Puritans along the Connecticut River formed the first colony. Other settlements joined later.

California	Spain	1769

FAST FACTS Spanish missionaries led the movement out of Mexico and into California.

Florida	Spain	1565

FAST FACTS Earlier Spanish and French forts did not survive. Great Britain took control in the 1700s and divided Florida into East and West Florida. Spain regained West Florida in 1783, but later sold it to the United States.

Georgia	England	1733

FAST FACTS Spain had missions in Georgia before the English arrived. For a time, slavery was illegal in the colony. James Oglethorpe, one of the founders, wanted poor whites to work there and better themselves.

Louisiana	France	1699

FAST FACTS The colony's main city, New Orleans, was founded in 1718. France gave Louisiana to Spain during the French and Indian War.

Maryland	England	1634

FAST FACTS The Calvert family, who were Roman Catholic, ruled Maryland for most of the 1600s.

Massachusetts	England	1620

FAST FACTS In 1692 the separate colonies of Plymouth and Massachusetts Bay united to form Massachusetts. Maine was a part of Massachusetts until 1820.

New France (Canada)	France	1608

FAST FACTS The first major French settlement was at Quebec. From there, merchants traded with Native Americans for furs.

New Hampshire	England	1623

FAST FACTS New Hampshire briefly shared a governor with Massachusetts, and some of its land later became part of Vermont.

COLONY	FOUNDED BY	YEAR
New Jersey	England	1664

FAST FACTS For a time, New Jersey was split into East and West Jersey; the two colonies were united in 1702.

New Mexico	Spain	1598

FAST FACTS The colony originally included Texas and Arizona as well as present-day New Mexico.

New Netherland	The Netherlands	1614

FAST FACTS Conquered by the English in 1664; New York City was the main British base during the American Revolution.

New Sweden (Delaware)	Sweden	1638

FAST FACTS Conquered by the Netherlands in 1655, many of its first settlers came from Finland.

North Carolina	England	1663

FAST FACTS In the 1500s, Spanish and English settlements failed. The first permanent settlers emigrated from Virginia.

Pennsylvania	England	1681

FAST FACTS Founder William Penn, a Quaker, had good relations with local Native American tribes.

Rhode Island	England	1636

FAST FACTS Roger Williams left Massachusetts and founded Providence. It was one of four mini-colonies that united to form Rhode Island in 1644.

South Carolina	England	1663

FAST FACTS In the 1600s, Spanish and French settlements failed. The first group of permanent English settlers arrived from the island of Barbados.

Virginia	England	1607

FAST FACTS John Smith, an early leader of Virginia, wrote about Native American wars and his travels through the Chesapeake.

TIMELINE

1513 Spanish explorers reach Florida.

1565 Spain founds St. Augustine, its first permanent settlement in Florida.

1598 Spanish settlers enter New Mexico.

1607 English settlers found Jamestown, Virginia.

1608 Founding of Quebec, the first lasting French settlement in Canada.

1609 Jamestown settlers and Powhatan tribe fight the first of several wars.

1614 The Dutch build a fort along the Hudson River, near present-day Albany, New York.

1619 African Americans, either indentured servants or slaves, are brought to Virginia.

1620 Pilgrims land in Plymouth, Massachusetts.

1637 New England colonists defeat the Pequot tribe and enslave the survivors.

1655 The Dutch conquer New Sweden (Delaware).

1664 The English conquer New Netherland (New York, New Jersey, and Delaware).

1680 Pueblos of New Mexico rebel against the Spanish, briefly earning their independence.

1699 The French start their first permanent settlement in Louisiana.

1704 French and Native American forces raid Deerfield, Massachusetts.

1718 New Orleans is founded and soon becomes the major city in Louisiana.

1763 Great Britain wins the French and Indian War and receives almost all of France's North American lands east of the Mississippi; the British also obtain Florida.

1765 Americans protest the Stamp Act, which taxes paper goods and documents.

1767 Parliament passes the Townshend Acts, which place new taxes on the colonies.

1768 British troops arrive in Boston to prevent more protests.

1773 The Boston Tea Party occurs when Boston patriots protest a tea tax by throwing crates of tea into the harbor.

1775 British troops and Americans fight in Lexington and Concord, Massachusetts, in the first battles of the American Revolution.

1776 American colonies officially declare their independence from Great Britain.

1783 The American Revolution ends; the United States receives new land from Great Britain, extending its border to the Mississippi River.

1787 Congress creates the Northwest Territory, a region north of the Ohio River and west of the Mississippi.

GLOSSARY

adobe building material made out of dried mud and straw

ally person or country working with for a common goal, such as defeating an another enemy

border dividing line between one country or region and another

boycott refuse to buy certain goods, as a protest against a company or government

cash crop crop, such as tobacco, raised on large farms and sold in far-away markets

climate average weather conditions in a region over a long time

colony land not connected to a nation, yet owned and controlled by it

Congress part of the U.S. government that makes the country's laws

convert change people's current religion for a new one

corrupt tending to commit crimes and pursue only one's own interests

economy total goods ands services produced in a region

emigrate leave one country or region to live in another

fertile land that is good for growing crops

foundry factory where raw iron ore is turned into the metal iron

frontier largely unsettled border areas of a region or colony

indigo plant that produces a blue dye used to color cloth

investor person who gives money to a company, hoping to earn more in return

lice small insects that live on people or animals

mission church or other place where missionaries live or work

missionary someone who is sent by a church or religious group to teach that group's faith or do good works, especially in a foreign country

nutrient chemical in the ground that helps crops grow

Parliament branch of the British government that makes laws

patriot American colonist who opposed British policies during the 1770s and supported the American Revolution

plantation large farm where crops such as coffee, tea, rubber, or cotton are grown

politics affairs of a government and the people who choose it

Protestant Christian who rejected the teachings of the Roman Catholic Church and followed a new religion

repeal get rid of or end

representative person chosen by voters to speak out for their interests

settlement colony or group of people who have left one place to make a home in another

settler person who moves from one place into a new region

slave person forced to do work

treaty an agreement between countries or governments

West Indies group of islands southeast of the United States in the Caribbean Sea

FURTHER READING

BOOKS

Bial, Raymond. *The Wampanoag*. New York: Benchmark, 2004.

Bullock, Steven C. *The American Revolution: A History in Documents*. New York: Oxford University Press, 2003.

Burgan, Michael. *Colonial and Revolutionary Times*. New York: Franklin Watts, 2003.

Fischer, Laura. *Life in New Amsterdam*. Chicago: Heinemann Library, 2003.

Gard, Carolyn. *The French and Indian War: A Primary Source History of the Fight for Territory in North America*. New York: Rosen Central Primary Source, 2004.

McCarthy, Pat. *The Thirteen Colonies from Founding to Revolution in American History*. Berkeley Heights, N.J.: Enslow, 2004.

Press, Petra. *The Pueblo*. Minneapolis: Compass Point, 2001.

Slavicek, Louise Chipley. *Life Among the Puritans*. San Diego: Lucent, 2001.

Stefoff, Rebecca. *Colonial Life*. New York: Benchmark, 2003.

INTERNET

Colonial House
http://www.pbs.org/wnet/colonialhouse/

French Colonies in America
http://www.southalabama.edu/archaeology/fc-america.htm

From Colonies to Revolution
http://www.teacheroz.com/colonies.htm

Iroquois Indian Museum
http://www.iroquoismuseum.org/index.htm

Liberty! The American Revolution
http://www.pbs.org/ktca/liberty/index.html

Plimoth Plantation
http://www.plimoth.org

Religion and the Founding of the American Republic
http://www.loc.gov/exhibits/religion/rel01.html

Spanish Exploration and Conquest of Native America
http://www.floridahistory.com/

INDEX